Inspiring Creativity and Innovation in K–12

Douglas Reeves

Solution Tree | Press

Copyright © 2015 by Solution Tree Press

Materials appearing here are copyrighted. With one exception, all rights are reserved. Readers may reproduce only those pages marked "Reproducible." Otherwise, no part of this book may be reproduced or transmitted in any form or by any means (electronic, photocopying, recording, or otherwise) without prior written permission of the publisher.

555 North Morton Street
Bloomington, IN 47404
800.733.6786 (toll free) / 812.336.7700
FAX: 812.336.7790

email: info@solution-tree.com
solution-tree.com

Visit **go.solution-tree.com/technology** to download the reproducibles in this book.

Printed in the United States of America

19 18 17 16 15   2 3 4 5

Library of Congress Cataloging-in-Publication Data

Reeves, Douglas B., 1953-
  Inspiring creativity and innovation in K-12 / Douglas B. Reeves.
    pages cm
  Includes bibliographical references.
  ISBN 978-1-936765-30-0 (perfect bound) 1. Creative thinking--Study and teaching--United States. 2. Creative ability--Study and teaching--United States. 3. Creative thinking in children--United States. I. Title.
  LB1590.5.R44 2015
  370.15'70951249--dc23
                         2015008897

Solution Tree
Jeffrey C. Jones, CEO
Edmund M. Ackerman, President

Solution Tree Press
President: Douglas M. Rife
Associate Acquisitions Editor: Kari Gillesse
Editorial Director: Lesley Bolton
Managing Production Editor: Caroline Weiss
Senior Production Editor: Christine Hood
Proofreader: Elisabeth Abrams
Text and Cover Designer: Rian Anderson
Compositor: Rachel Smith

For Amy

Acknowledgments

One of the most important lessons in the study of creativity is that the myth of the lone genius is a particularly destructive one, leading us to believe that real creative endeavors are solitary. Work that acknowledges the assistance of others is, in one of the worst epithets that can be hurled in the academic community, merely "derivative." Writers not only have muses but also those who provide intellectual and emotional support that are essential to the production of every book.

Lauren Kruczkowski provided vital assistance in collecting an international sample of creativity rubrics and helped with their analysis. In addition, Lauren processed a decade of results on PLCs and helped to synthesize the data and render a complex and disparate sea of reports into a comprehensible set of data. In both cases, her efforts led to original research that is published for the first time in these pages. Brooks Reeves offered helpful comments on early drafts of the chapters and, in the course of vigorous discussions, helped to frame my thinking on this subject.

Readers can thank Christine Hood and her colleagues at Solution Tree Press for proving Stephen King's dictum that to write is human, to edit, divine. The book is shorter and more accessible because of their efforts. Douglas Rife, the president of Solution Tree Press, had the vision for a series of brief and focused books that bring complex topics to readers in a user-friendly format. Jeff Jones, the CEO of Solution Tree, leads an organization whose mission is to advance the work of its authors. Every author can only hope for the sort of supportive and intellectually challenging environment that Solution Tree provides.

The reference section is woefully insufficient to acknowledge my debt to the authors on whose research and wisdom I depend. I must nevertheless single out for special appreciation Mihaly Csikszentmihalyi, Richard DuFour, Howard Gardner, John Hattie, and Grant Wiggins.

Although I am grateful for the people listed in the foregoing paragraphs, the inevitable errors and omissions are mine alone.

Douglas Reeves
Boston, Massachusetts

Visit **go.solution-tree.com/technology** to download the reproducibles in this book.

Table of Contents

About the Author... ix

Chapter 1: Why Creativity Is Vital 1

Creative Discomfort... 2

Delayed Feedback... 3

Abdication of Authority....................................... 4

Disciplinary Silos... 5

Chapter 2: Building a Creative Culture.....................7

Mistake-Tolerant Culture...................................... 7

Rigorous Decision-Making System 11

Culture That Nurtures Creativity 12

Leadership Team That Models and Supports Creativity....... 13

Creative Environment Rubric 15

**Chapter 3: How Educators and Leaders Discourage
Creativity**... **19**

Practices That Undermine Creativity.......................... 20

Rarely Give Students Unfettered Rein 21

Offer Creative Work to Students as a Reward................. 22

Focus on Individual Rather Than Group Work 23

Use Brainstorming as the Best Way to Generate New Ideas....24

Demand That Student Work Is Right the First Time 24

Insist That Creative Work Is Immune From Evaluation and
Criticism... 25

Avoid Assessment of Creativity..............................26
Attitudes and Beliefs That Undermine Creativity..............26
    Creativity Is a Natural Talent or Gift..........................26
    Real Creative Work Is Distinctly Original 27
    Creativity Cannot Happen Without Inspiration 29
    Left-Brain and Right-Brain Differences Heavily Influence
        Creativity 30
    Creative Inspiration Is Like Lightning 31
Standards of Evidence.......................................32
    Personal Beliefs 32
    Personal Experience 32
    Collective Experience 33
    Systematic Observation 33
    Preponderance of Evidence.................................34

Chapter 4: How Educators and Leaders Can Encourage Creativity 35
    Eight Dimensions of Creativity Assessment 36
    The Current State of Creativity Assessment 39
    Metarubric for Assessing Creativity Rubrics.................43

Chapter 5: Adapting the Four Essential Questions of PLCs to Creativity 49
    PLCs and Achievement 51
    Using the Four Essential Questions to Enhance Creativity
        and Achievement 53

Chapter 6: Creativity for Education Policymakers........ 59
    Inclusion...60
    Collaboration 61
    Debate, Dissent, and Discipline in Decision Making..........62
    Accountability 63
    Forgiveness 63

References and Resources 65

About the Author

 **Douglas Reeves** is a partner with Creative Leadership Solutions, serving education systems around the world. The author of more than thirty books and eighty articles on leadership and education, he has been named twice to the Harvard University Distinguished Author Series, received the Contribution to the Field Award from the National Staff Development Council (now Learning Forward), and was named the Brock International Laureate for his contributions to education. He is the founding publisher of the *SNAFU Review*, a literary and artistic project supporting disabled veterans whose writing and art inspire others struggling with post-traumatic stress disorder.

To learn more about Doug's work, visit http://creativeleadership.net or follow him on Twitter @DouglasReeves.

To book Douglas Reeves for professional development, contact pd@solution-tree.com.

Chapter 1
Why Creativity Is Vital

Sir Ken Robinson's writing (2014) and wildly popular YouTube videos (thirty million hits and counting) make clear the importance of creativity for the future of the planet. Creativity is the first priority in talent selection by the Global CEO Study (Lombardo & Roddy, 2010), finishing higher in that survey than integrity and global thinking. Creativity is foundational to human progress, scientific endeavors, and educational success. In the best synthesis of the international evidence, Heather Hammond and colleagues (2013) and John Hattie (2012) find durable positive relationships between creativity and student achievement and conclude that successful nurturing of creativity depends on feedback that is accurate and active.

The fundamental question is this: Why do so many people enthusiastically watch a Ken Robinson video and devour research about creativity and achievement and then do absolutely nothing about what they learned? This book explores the challenges of creativity and offers practical advice for educators, school leaders, and policymakers. It is not enough to acknowledge that creativity is important; we must first understand why creativity presents such a challenge, particularly in an educational environment.

The quest for creativity presents four central challenges to education professionals and students. First, creativity is risky and uncomfortable. Second, creativity fails to offer the immediate positive feedback to which generations of students have become accustomed. Few students persist in the face of failure—the inevitable result of creative efforts. Third, the abdication of authority by teachers is worrisome to teachers, students, parents, and administrators. Fourth is the challenge of disciplinary silos. Despite abundant evidence that the development of creativity depends on interdisciplinary efforts, faculty members, particularly at secondary and collegiate levels, find the greatest professional and psychological security within the academic disciplines where their expertise is unchallenged.

Creative Discomfort

Risk, failure, and ambiguity—these are among the essential ingredients of creativity. Yet while there is nearly unanimous praise for the concept of creativity, there is little enthusiasm for the difficult, challenging, and sometimes embarrassing steps required to achieve the goal. Prolific inventor James Dyson (2000) estimates that he experienced more than five thousand failures before developing the eponymous vacuum cleaner that now dominates the industry. Stories of successful ideas go back centuries to the time of Archimedes, who is credited with the original "Eureka!" moment, sitting in his bathtub pondering a challenge from the king. But it's a good bet that Archimedes took a lot of baths before yelling "Eureka!" as he ran naked through the town, proclaiming his discovery of water displacement by irregularly shaped objects.

Discomfort is not, however, part of most school environments, where students and teachers are encouraged to "get it right the first time." The common use of the average—the default of most computerized evaluation systems when summarizing a set of scores—means that the risk, experimentation, and discomfort experienced during the first days of school are part of final student and teacher evaluations. Even the Global CEO Study finds that while 60 percent of leaders claim to value creativity as one of the primary attributes of leaders they hire, more than 70 percent admit that they do a poor job of assessing and encouraging it (Lombardo & Roddy, 2010). In the business world, it's difficult to engage in creative discomfort when your bonus as well as your mortgage payment depend on tomorrow's results.

In education, creative ways of engaging students give way to the exigencies of tomorrow's test. For example, one of the best ways to encourage creativity is with an environment of debate and dissent (Rogers & Simms, 2014). Yet this promising instructional strategy is often doomed by a culture of congeniality in which respecting one's classmates and colleagues is interpreted by some students and teachers as never engaging in open disagreement, dissent, or criticism.

Delayed Feedback

Compare the following profiles of the performance of two students. Each student submitted ten projects, assignments, or other assessments for teacher evaluation. Both students finished the class doing A work, but there the similarity ends.

Student 1: A, A, A, A, A, A, A, B, A, A—Final grade of A

Student 2: F, F, F, A, F, F, F, A, F, A—Final grade?

The first student knows the game of school well. As close to failure and risk taking as the first student comes is to receive a B—a rare occurrence that may lead to challenges for the teacher from both student and parents. The language of the grade doesn't matter—whether the mark is B or "meets expectations"—the perception, at least in many affluent homes, is that a score less than perfection is a dagger in the heart of a student who is accustomed to only receiving the highest marks available.

The second student swings for the fences, alternating between spectacular failure and success. With a rare degree of resilience, the second student willingly persists in the face of failure after failure, rewarded by the occasional success. Colleges, graduate schools, and employers insist that they value creativity and risk taking, but which student are they more likely to accept or hire? It's tempting to be cynical about grade inflation among students. However, the same issue presents itself when superintendents routinely meet or exceed the expectations of the boards that hired them and, even in an environment of renewed evaluation and accountability, the vast majority of teachers receive high ratings.

Abdication of Authority

Take it from a parent who has a very difficult time reconciling evidence about risk and error with the reality that error, at least in an environment of high expectations and exceptional academic achievement, rarely occurs. When my daughter makes a scientific pronouncement that is clearly preposterous, I wonder, "Why didn't her teachers *teach* her the right way? They are supposed to be the experts!" However, whenever she parrots something she has learned in school with insufficient critical reasoning, I wonder, "Why didn't her teachers let her *explore alternatives and challenge prevailing authority?*" I can't have it both ways, and teachers can't win in an environment in which parents simultaneously demand student creativity and conformity. We are caught in what might be called Gardner's Dilemma, after Harvard psychologist and Project Zero founder Howard Gardner. He makes a clarion call for both creativity and disciplinary excellence. To sum it up, you can't think outside of the box if you don't first *understand the box.*

Gardner's (1993) analysis of the creative processes of Freud, Einstein, Picasso, Stravinsky, Eliot, Graham, and Gandhi suggests that wildly diverse thinkers and artists share some common characteristics. Attributing their work to genius alone undermines the historical facts: they studied their craft, worked incredibly hard, and suffered many failures along the road to their success. If these magnificent thinkers had been evaluated on the average of their work, then Einstein would have retired in the Swiss patent office, and Stravinsky would have died on the streets of Paris trying to sell the shoes thrown at him during the premiere of *The Rite of Spring*.

Disciplinary Silos

Few secondary school administrators understand calculus as well as the mathematics teacher, fugues as well as the music teacher, literature and composition as well as the English teacher, history as well as the social studies teacher, or chemistry as well as the science teacher. Even with experience in teaching the primary grades, few elementary school administrators understand how to teach the essentials of reading, even though they are among the most important instructional skills required in the early grades. Because administrators cannot be experts in everything, it is reasonable to expect education leaders to be attuned to opportunities for meaningful collaboration among the faculty. For example, feedback strategies of the chorus conductor and athletic coach might inform their colleagues' professional practices in literacy and mathematics. Similarly, secondary school teachers whose students struggle with literacy can learn much from their colleagues who specialize in literacy instruction.

These four challenges—the risk and discomfort inherent in the creative process, students' need for immediate positive feedback, the abdication of authority by educators and leaders, and the persistence of disciplinary silos—militate against what we know to be essential progress toward creativity. These challenges are not met with an instruction manual or an academic study but rather with educators willing to build a creative culture. That is the focus of the next chapter.

Chapter 2
Building a Creative Culture

It does little good to encourage student creativity unless leaders have first put in place the essential elements of a creative environment. This chapter suggests four such essentials and offers a Creative Environment Rubric (see pages 16–18), so you and your colleagues can begin a quest to save creativity at your school with some objective analysis. These four essential elements include:

1. Mistake-tolerant culture

2. Rigorous decision-making system

3. Culture that nurtures creativity

4. Leadership team that models and supports creativity

Mistake-Tolerant Culture

The first element of a creative environment is a mistake-tolerant culture. Although much has been written and said about the value of mistakes in pursuing creativity, the practical reality is that in most schools, mistakes by students, teachers, and administrators are systematically punished. The least effective creative environments require blind compliance with rules and expectations. Success in these environments is equated with avoiding mistakes. The clear, if unspoken, leadership theme is this: We've worked too hard to get where we are to mess it up with any new ideas. Alan Deutschman (2007), in the compelling book *Change or Die*, writes that over decades of research, a consistent finding reveals that many people would rather die than make significant changes in their lives. The best evidence for such an over-the-top assertion is that more than 90 percent of people who have had open-heart surgery, often due to behavioral decisions such as smoking and a sedentary lifestyle, only briefly change the behaviors that landed them under the surgeon's knife. Within less than a year, they return to their old lifestyle. They would literally rather die than change.

In the field of education, I am often asked, "If it's so obvious, then why don't people just *do it?*" It is obvious, for example, that frequent feedback leads to better student results, but the vast majority of schools only provide students with meaningful feedback three or four times a year. To do more—certainly to provide feedback on a weekly basis—would leave teachers and administrators open to the complaint of "too much testing," an assertion that seems to shut down the argument. Imagine if diabetics refused to test their blood sugar level because such an effort involved too much testing.

More than two decades of research, from 1990 onward, demonstrate the strong link between writing and student performance in a variety of academic disciplines. One of the foremost researchers in this area, Professor Steve Graham of Vanderbilt University (2009–2010), documents not only the academic impact of writing but also the value of handwriting. Yet at both the K–12 and collegiate levels, the amount of writing required of students is declining (Arum & Roksa, 2010). Cursive writing is nearly extinct from public school settings, and most prevailing English language arts standards have abandoned the practice.

The zeal by students, parents, and teachers for immediate mastery requires that students quickly acquire and master new skills. This expectation would never be applied to proficiency in music or all but the simplest athletic endeavors. Only using what Hattie (2012) calls *deliberative practice* yields improved performance. However, applying this fundamental learning principle is systematically ignored in a culture in which mistakes—the essential building blocks of deliberative practice—receive negative reactions. Only in a school that actively opposes effective practice would you find the definition of *perfect homework* or *perfect project work* that is free from errors.

Lest this book appears to criticize students who have been taught to use negative feedback and mistakes to fuel their improvement, it's important to acknowledge that these students learned well from their adult role models. It's difficult to argue that self-esteem isn't a good thing; indeed, without a sufficient quantity of self-esteem, people lose the confidence to learn. However, the concept of self-esteem has been distorted from a healthy sense of confidence and personal efficacy—the sense that one can influence results with learning and hard work. In common school parlance, self-esteem is the product of endless reassurance from adults that children are almost perfect and nearly incapable of making mistakes. The social harmony of "you're awesome, I'm awesome, we're awesome" rarely gives way to the counterpoint of "I know I can do better if I work harder." But one of the most difficult things for many students (and parents) to hear is: "You can do better if you work harder." It requires a courageous teacher who is willing to give candid and critical feedback to students and withstand the possible withering assault of emails from parents.

Consider how many teaching and learning initiatives are rolled out in schools. These efforts, however well intended, are often more characterized by announcements, labels, and speeches than substantive changes in professional practice. The culture declares victory and moves on rather than expose new ideas to systematic evaluation. As a result, most student, teacher, and administrator evaluations focus on compliance, often with checklists, to ensure that participants in the system follow the rules and stray from the constraints at peril of their grades and careers. Compliance involves homework, attendance, and obedience, ensuring that even the best practices in research-based instruction are strangled in observations and evaluations.

The tension among three types of feedback—(1) effective feedback, (2) paralyzing feedback, and (3) benign feedback—leads to what Hammond and colleagues (2013) refer to as the Goldilocks Principle. When feedback is overbearing and punitive, it inhibits performance by everyone in the system, including students, educators, and administrators. But when feedback is absent or dully reassuring, it also has a negative effect, leaving the recipients endlessly wondering if they are really doing good work. Just as Goldilocks searched for the "just right" bowl of porridge, the development of a creative culture requires feedback that is accurate, specific, and timely but also humane and decent.

Feedback for students and teachers can be clear and explicit, and the best formats provide a continuum so that everyone in the school understands how to achieve a higher level of performance. For example, classroom protocols as seemingly obvious as "raise your hand before you speak" could be readily challenged if teachers and students were to consider other means of achieving recognition. Yet the 18th century protocol of raising one's hand to seek teacher recognition has been handed down from classroom to classroom, as if it were sacred fire rather than an outmoded system of engaging students in thoughtful conversations. Kim Marshall (2014) provides an excellent way to coach teachers on effective feedback techniques by providing a clear continuum of descriptions of professional practices. His rubric for monitoring, assessment, and follow-up includes the following range of professional practices.

- **Highly Effective:** Uses a variety of effective methods to check for understanding; immediately unscrambles confusion and clarifies

- **Effective:** Frequently checks for understanding and gives students helpful information if they seem confused

- **Improvement Necessary:** Uses mediocre methods (such as thumbs-up, thumbs-down) to check for understanding during instruction

- **Does Not Meet Standards:** Uses ineffective methods (for example, "Is everyone with me?") to check for understanding

Students can also be very helpful in creating a range of performance standards. Larry Ainsworth (1998) makes a compelling case for the clarity and specificity provided by student-generated rubrics. He calls it the *playground standard* of clarity. When students explain the rules of a game to one another, they don't use complex or obscure language. They say, "You can go *here*, but you can't go *there*. You can do *this*, but you can't do *that*." Few kindergarteners I know have arrived home and gleefully exclaimed, "Mommy, I did great in phonemic awareness today!" Yet many report cards continue to use language that alienates parents and is unclear to students. If feedback for students or adults in the school is to have an impact on performance, then it must be clear to the giver as well as the receiver.

Rigorous Decision-Making System

The second essential element of a creative environment is a rigorous decision-making system. This kind of environment embraces discussion and debate as the fundamental processes for decision making on everything from class rules to criteria for student success to leadership and board policies. This is the opposite of student success defined by a teacher's syllabus and rubrics and teacher and leadership success defined as compliance with a voluminous scorecard. Indeed, most board policy discussions are not conducted in an atmosphere of discussion and debate but rather behind closed doors from which a single recommendation is forwarded to the board for (almost inevitable) acceptance or rejection.

Alan Lafley and Roger Martin (2013) set a very high standard for disciplined decision making. They require decision makers to have mutually exclusive alternatives. In contrast to the common practice of presenting a single recommendation for consideration, they require alternatives, debate, and clear acceptance of one alternative and rejection of others. This is effective guidance not only for the board-room but also for the classroom. The search for comity that infects so many social situations, including the classroom, is the enemy of vigorous debate and rigorous analysis of alternatives. When students believe that the end of every debate results in both sides being right, they arrive to the world outside of school better prepared for cocktail party conversation than a position of responsibility.

This approach to decision making is not just plucked from the business world and forced on schools. The concept of competing, mutually exclusive decision alternatives is essential in many environments, including nonprofit boards, religious institutions, schools, and symphony orchestras. I once watched James Levine conduct a rehearsal of the Boston Symphony. He asked different musicians for their opinions on the sound and expressive qualities of a particular passage. Although the musicians seemed pleased to have their opinions solicited, they also understood that Levine would consider the alternatives and then make a decision. Rigorous decision making, whether it is the opinion of a story in second grade or a multimillion-dollar technology proposal before a school board, requires that advocates take a position, defend it, critique alternatives, and then understand that, win or lose, they contributed to a culture in which dissent is not a social evil to avoid but a creative imperative to embrace.

Culture That Nurtures Creativity

The third essential element of a creative culture is a culture that nurtures creativity. Certainly it would be difficult to find a school or education system that does not claim to value and encourage creativity. However, the purpose of this chapter is to separate perception from reality. For example, it is a laudable goal in many schools to have a high-reliability system, that is, a school in which similar efforts yield similar results. This concept works fine . . . until it doesn't. Rather than pride itself primarily on its consistency, a school with an environment that nurtures creativity can provide a variety of case studies demonstrating how dissent and divergent thinking are welcome.

Science fairs (and, more importantly, science classes) applaud students who express hypotheses, test them, and reject them. Student writers don't welcome requirements for writing four or five drafts of an essay until they are able to personally see the difference between the first and final drafts. Leaders in a creative culture recognize creativity not only in art class but also in every student endeavor, from the athletic field to mathematics class to faculty meetings. Science fairs are not just for students; they are a remarkably effective way to encourage creativity among teachers (Reeves, 2008). Teachers need not write dissertations to conduct credible research that influences professional practice. Just as student science fair displays typically are presented on a three-panel display board, the adult science fair display is a simplified version, with the headings:

1. What was the challenge?

2. What did we do?

3. What were the results?

Although there are no awards or ribbons in the adult science fair, it creates a fun and nonthreatening environment in which professionals can share data with one another. For examples of how this was done successfully at every grade level, see *Reframing Teacher Leadership to Improve Your School* (Reeves, 2008).

An individual classroom experience is merely an anecdote; however, when dozens, even hundreds, of display boards are in the same room, an objective observer can begin to draw conclusions about the effective and ineffective practices in that particular environment. In building a culture of creativity, it is particularly important that displays of information are neither triumphant nor confessional—they are just facts presented by professionals for professionals.

Leadership Team That Models and Supports Creativity

The fourth essential element for nurturing a creative environment is a leadership team that models and supports creativity. Leaders model the essentials of creativity when, for example, they regularly talk about their mistakes and what they learned from them. They follow the model in Richard Elmore's (2011) book *I Used to Think . . . And Now I Think . . .* Although this sounds like an exercise in theory, actually applying this model can be a bit discouraging. Elmore's central idea can be applied to a three-column chart—the left column titled, "I used to think . . .," the middle column titled, "Now I think . . .," and the right column titled, "I changed because . . ." Most people can think of ways they have changed their thinking about all kinds of subjects, including history, science, or economics. It's not important that everyone agrees, but it's vital that people determine one way they have changed their thinking.

Many times, I have been in front of a roomful of school and system leaders and challenged them to think of something that they knew was certainly true when they were in college but is not true today. The most common response is silence. "Nothing?" I ask. "Not a single research claim, not a single staff development fad?" When prodded, these leaders begin thinking of a few mistakes—advocated by others and revealed as bogus on further reflection. But when they are pressed to find something that they believed sincerely but that they no longer believe, it makes for some very awkward moments in professional learning. Attempting to lead by example, I offer some of my own beliefs that I have had to discard over the years. For example, I used to believe that it was self-evident that students tended to one of three learning styles—visual, auditory, or kinesthetic. I thought that teachers should be able to diagnose which learning style was prevalent for each of their students and then make an active effort to teach toward that particular learning style. I also used to believe that the theory of multiple intelligences stood in stark contrast to the need for high academic standards for all students.

As in many cases, I was wrong on both counts. Neuropsychologist Daniel Willingham (2010) and researcher Hattie (2012) decimate learning styles theory, demonstrating that when teachers attempt to diagnose a particular learning style, they do so inconsistently to the point that the "diagnosis" has no meaning. Moreover, when teachers attempt to teach to a particular learning style, the students who are supposed to benefit from this strategy demonstrate no better performance than students who are taught differently. Finally, my comeuppance on the theory of multiple intelligences comes from Gardner (1999), who kindly inscribed a copy of his book by writing emphatically:

> A belief in multiple intelligences . . . is in no sense a statement about standards, rigor, or expectations, and it is certainly not a rejection of these desiderata. On the contrary: I am a demon for high standards and demanding expectations. . . . It pains me to see my work aligned (I could have written "maligned") with that of individuals who are apologists for low extenders, low expectations, "anything goes." (p. 25)

Actually reading Gardner's work rather than believing in false summaries of his work by true believers carries a certain peril, as does acknowledging errors, which is so essential for establishing a creative environment. What is the response from leaders who witness someone acknowledge error and change his or her views because of newly learned evidence? "Thank you for your honesty and credibility" would be a nice start. But that's not the most common reaction. Public and sometimes anonymous critics consistently say, "If you were wrong ten years ago, why should we believe you today?" If this is the model that leaders establish, then we cannot be surprised when the entire school or education system is impervious to change. New evidence, no matter how powerful, is sometimes an insufficient force to change people and institutions that equate a change in view with mental frailty and professional weakness.

There is, fortunately, a way out of this destructive cycle of confident assertion followed by ineffective professional practices that are resistant to evidence-based change. We can create a systematic way of assessing each one of the essentials of a creative culture.

Creative Environment Rubric

The Creative Environment Rubric in figure 2.1 (pages 16–18) will help you to identify phrases that describe your school or system.

Most often, you will find that your school or system does not fit neatly into one category, but it fits in parts of different levels of creative performance.

Essential Element 1: Mistake-Tolerant Culture	
Novice	Our culture requires compliance. Success is equated with avoiding mistakes. Our culture claims, "We've worked too hard to get to where we are to mess it up with any new ideas."
Developing	Initiatives are more characterized by announcements, labels, and speeches than substantive changes in professional practice. Our culture declares victory and moves on rather than expose new ideas to systematic evaluation.
Proficient	Within the past year, at least two specific ideas were welcomed as potentially worthy, subjected to rigorous experimentation, and then rejected—all without negative consequences to the backers of those ideas.
Exemplary	Learning mistakes—errors that test hypotheses and find them to be wrong—are visibly celebrated. We embrace a bone-deep belief that a zero-mistake zone is a zero-learning zone.
Essential Element 2: Rigorous Decision-Making System	
Novice	The leader decides, and our team implements. If someone else has a different opinion, he or she is not considered a team player with adequate buy-in. We believe that the recalcitrant faculty member can be fixed with an inspirational speaker.
Developing	We listen to presentations from competing vendors and come to a consensus about our decisions. We tried coaching for a couple of years, followed by professional learning communities (PLCs), followed by positive behavior support, and then followed by academic vocabulary. However, none of these seemed to stick very well, so now we're looking for something that will finally work for us.

Proficient	Before we make important decisions about teaching, learning, curriculum, assessment, or leadership, we consider at least two alternatives and use the best available evidence from a variety of sources and methods.
Exemplary	We always consider at least two mutually exclusive hypotheses and test them with data. We know what works and what doesn't work because we test alternatives. As new data emerge, we are willing to change our views. We never pile one solution on top of another, but instead, we apply logical considerations of alternatives. We believe that if X is true, then Y cannot be true, so it doesn't make any sense to adopt both X and Y.
Essential Element 3: Culture That Nurtures Creativity	
Novice	We are a research-based system. We know what works, and we deliver that product— student learning—in a consistently effective way based on decades of experience and research. We are not interested in people experimenting with our students.
Developing	When we make changes, we do so "around the edges." Our fundamental mission, vision, and values are "untouchables," and whatever changes we make must be made without violating our sacred traditions.
Proficient	We can identify a significant change that was studied, debated, implemented, tested, and stood the test of time through constant rigorous assessment.
Exemplary	We have many case studies, modeled on well-recognized, creative successes in music, art, engineering, teaching, learning, and leadership. Our students and staff have the discipline to start with repetition and the courage to experiment creatively with new ideas.

Figure 2.1: Creative environment rubric.   Continued →

Essential Element 4: Leadership Team That Models and Supports Creativity	
Novice	We might try some initiatives, such as implementing new technology, but that's for the Geek Squad, not busy leaders. When it's all working perfectly, the leaders take a look—but not until there is no risk of public embarrassment.
Developing	Leaders are masters of the rhetoric of change. They have posters on the virtues of innovation and creativity in their offices, and they return from conferences inspired by futuristic thinking, typically framed in vague phrases and evidence-free predictions.
Proficient	Leaders know that creative ideas lack credibility without visible leadership support. At least a couple of times in the past year, leaders personally modeled a change before it was implemented throughout the organization.
Exemplary	Leaders are actively engaged in experimentation, including flipping agendas for board meetings and personally engaging in alternative learning and teaching strategies. Leaders openly talk about their biggest mistakes and what they learned from them.

Now that you have a clearer idea of how your school or system is working its way toward an environment that nurtures creativity, let's consider how schools, often intermittently, can undermine creativity.

Chapter 3

How Educators and Leaders Discourage Creativity

At the end of a long holiday weekend, the airport was crowded with frustrated passengers. Their planes were delayed, their kids were hungry, and the crankiest of all were not the babies but their weary and fractious parents. As I worked at a small table in the waiting area, I noticed that some clever airport managers had created a small putting green to occupy bored fliers. Three children had taken over the course. They were four, five, and six years old (I had overheard them introducing themselves by grade, age, school, and hometown). For a while, they tried to use the golf clubs to play golf. But the motor skills required to knock the ball into the hole soon grew too challenging, so the youngest suggested, "Let's play hockey!" Soon, all three were wielding their new "hockey sticks" with delight. Some time later, another child suggested, "Let's play soccer!" Abandoning their clubs, they started kicking a golf ball from one end of the course to the other. Eventually, a parent looked up to see what was happening and exclaimed, "My goodness! Look at how spontaneously creative these children are, even under these aggravating conditions!" Of course he didn't say that. "This is a golf course!" he firmly intoned, "and you're going to damage it!" Within seconds, the children had stopped playing, and they returned to looks of boredom and despair, no longer inventing their own games to relieve the anxiety of the situation but waiting as we all were for the flight to finally take off.

Children are not always the heroes of airline terminal stories. They can be impatient and loud, stretched out over three or four waiting-area seats as they sink into the oblivion of video games and cell phones. But these kids were minding their own business, relieving their parents and other passengers of other possible mischief. The point is that sometimes even when children are creative in a thoughtful, social, productive, and cooperative way, we can fail to recognize it and also unwittingly undermine it.

Creativity can be undermined by seven teaching and leadership practices and five attitudes and beliefs. None of these practices or attitudes begins with the desire to diminish creativity. Indeed, teachers embrace some of these practices and attitudes with the best of intentions. But however good the intent may be, these practices and attitudes can have a dulling impact on student creativity. It is essential to distinguish practices from attitudes. The reason is that many people express positive attitudes about creativity, while still continuing to use practices that undermine it. For example, almost every school claims to value creativity among its staff and students, but its evaluation system punishes experimentation and risk taking.

Practices That Undermine Creativity

There is a delicate balance between providing clear and unequivocal feedback (a practice strongly associated with learning) and delivering a scathing critical judgment (a practice that undermines learning and paralyzes learners). By identifying unproductive practices, with gentleness and respect, we can lay the groundwork for establishing a learning environment that nourishes and encourages creativity.

Rarely Give Students Unfettered Rein

There are two seemingly contradictory themes in contemporary education policy debates. The first is that creativity is an essential 21st century skill. The second is that academic standards, although flawed in their implementation, represent the best way to assess student performance. Partisans of both themes sometimes cast them as polar opposites. One extreme is the view that Common Core standards, or any other set of academic standards, suppress creativity (Zhao, 2014). The other extreme is that creativity is a frill that must be pushed to the periphery until students first meet the standards. But the best synthesis of evidence, including case studies, quantitative analysis, meta-analysis, and synthesis of meta-analysis, leads to the conclusion that standards and creativity are not mutually exclusive but mutually reinforcing.

Who would you guess wrote the following statement? "Creation is unlikely to emerge in the absence of some disciplinary mastery and, perhaps, some capacity to synthesize; it's not possible to think outside the box unless you have a box." Who would make such a claim? Some bloggers, who obviously do not support the use of academic standards, might claim that any advocate of disciplinary mastery is obviously a captive of the corporate-educational complex and is indifferent to the interests of students and the importance of creativity. They might be surprised to learn that the author of this quote is one of the leading advocates of creativity in our time, Howard Gardner (2009, p. 17), in his wonderful book *Five Minds for the Future*. A thoughtful and self-effacing scholar, Gardner cautions his readers about the dangers of concluding that his theory of multiple intelligences has been thoroughly tested. He encourages further research and hypothesis testing that form the essence of good research. In his writings, he is a staunch advocate for rigorous standards and objective testing of theoretical claims. If Gardner can find common ground between the demands for creativity and academic standards, then so should the rest of us.

Are there flaws in academic standards, including the Common Core standards? Certainly. But let's remember what the alternatives really are. The alternative to standards is not some education utopia in which students and teachers magically find the path to optimal learning. The choice is stark. If you dislike standards, then learn to love the bell curve. Education institutions either compare students to an objective standard, as we commonly do for our most demanding professions, or we compare students to one another. The latter choice, the bell curve or normal distribution, is especially pernicious. It validates the performance of lower-performing students ("You're not really proficient, but at least you beat the kids across town!") and invalidates the performance of excellent students ("You might have excellent performance, but some kid across town beat you!"). The bell curve is the world of bluebirds, robins, and blackbirds—no accident in the choice of colors. In the 1960s, student reading groups would bear these sorts of labels. While the labels may have changed, the impetus for students and their parents to revel in competition rather than achievement remains a dominant theme in many schools and classrooms. Standards are the path to fairness and equity. Most importantly, as Gardner (1999) suggests, when we insist that students achieve disciplinary excellence, we open the door to their creative pursuits.

In sum, we can do better than the contemporary political debates in which one extreme is pitted against another. We can find a reasonable middle ground that includes both embracing the creative efforts of students and teachers and committing to disciplinary excellence. We can, in brief, think outside the box and also understand the box.

Offer Creative Work to Students as a Reward

Summarizing data from the U.S. Department of Education, the Association of American Educators (2012) reports that arts programs around the country have declined significantly, with the greatest declines in drama. Schools that are economically disadvantaged are most likely to experience a reduction in their arts programs. It is no coincidence that this decline took place during a period in which the economic survival of administrators—perhaps of the entire school—was based on best scores in literacy and mathematics.

Thus, some administrators seemed to see time as a zero-sum game in which any time devoted to music instruction or drama experiences was considered stolen from the study of mandatory academic curriculum. The practice of discarding the arts in favor of reading and mathematics might make sense if one believed that these are mutually exclusive subjects. But anyone who has watched a great music teacher in action can see the connection of musical and mathematical thinking—everything from the elements of counting to more complex ratios. Sometimes this musical invitation, with rhythm, sound, and movement, is more engaging than tables and formulas. Experiences in drama require not only the ability to read but also to understand a character's point of view and his or her relationship with the scene, plot, and other characters. This is precisely the sort of complex interpretation that students must have to succeed in literacy assessments.

Focus on Individual Rather Than Group Work

Almost every teacher and group member has encountered the folly of poorly designed work groups. In some cases, a whole group is unsuccessful due to the laziness or incompetence of one group member. In other cases, a single group member, perhaps fearing low marks due to the indolence of another group member, completes almost all the work, ensuring a high score but denying other members meaningful participation in the group. "Why bother?" The teacher shrugs. "Contrived collaboration seems less like a 21st century skill than medieval gamesmanship, and I don't have time for that in my classroom. Besides, my most creative students just need to be left alone to create." The myth of the lone creative genius is an attractive one, but it fails to square with the evidence about how creativity works. Creativity most likely emerges from teams, whether the context is the dawn of the Impressionist movement in Paris or the latest technological innovations. As Alex Pentland (2014) notes in *Social Physics: How Good Ideas Spread—The Lessons From a New Science*, "In research labs and in design shops, the difference between low-creative groups and high-creative groups is their pattern of face-to-face exploration outside of the group, together with their engagement within the group" (p. 96).

Group work can be frustrating and often maddening, particularly when compared to the solitary bliss of individual contemplation. The problem is that what is most comfortable is not necessarily most conducive to creative endeavors. Collaboration requires work and, sometimes, difficult interpersonal interactions. However, compared to the myth of the lone genius, collaboration is far more effective in producing creative results.

Use Brainstorming as the Best Way to Generate New Ideas

In 2014, Creative Leadership Solutions conducted the *International Study of Creativity Rubrics*, a review of more than one hundred assessments of student creative processes and results. In that study, we found that one of the most common errors was a reliance on brainstorming, a long discredited pseudointellectual process in which group members throw out ideas in the absence of criticism, evaluation, or reflection. The original scheme for brainstorming, developed by advertising executive Alex Osborn in 1948, called for an environment in which the primary rule of group discussion was "no criticism." Although university studies dating from 1960 conclude that brainstorming is ineffective, it remained in vogue for decades and is a fixture of creativity assessments (Osborn, 1976). A far more effective strategy for generating creative ideas is a process in which students first work alone and then share their ideas with fellow students, welcoming criticism and evaluation. Groups that engage in this process, as opposed to traditional brainstorming, generate more ideas of greater quality that, even weeks later, are more likely to be implemented.

Demand That Student Work Is Right the First Time

The demands of school schedules and the traditions of homework and testing have created an environment in which there is an imperative to get it right the first time. The aversion to risk inherent in this philosophy leads students and teachers to avoid risk taking, pursue the path of least resistance, and submit perfunctory, satisfactory, and entirely uncreative work.

Insist That Creative Work Is Immune From Evaluation and Criticism

It's difficult to embrace evaluation and criticism in an age of narcissism. Difficult but necessary. In *The Narcissism Epidemic: Living in the Age of Entitlement*, Jean Twenge and Keith Campbell (2010) review data from eighty-five surveys published between 1979 and 2006, in which sixteen thousand university students completed the Narcissistic Personality Inventory. Narcissism scores rose progressively over almost three decades in the study. If the mythological story of Narcissus fails to provide a sufficient evidentiary foundation for why self-absorption is a bad idea, then the best evidence to the contrary is that critical evaluation—the bane of narcissism—is essential to promoting creativity. In one of the definitive works on the subject of creativity, *Creativity: The Psychology of Discovery and Invention*, Mihaly Csikszentmihalyi (1996) writes about scores of creative people from the 20th century who embraced important ideas to inform their 21st century descendants. One common theme among scientists, novelists, artists, Nobel laureates, and many others is that they welcome divergent thinking, dissent, debate, and criticism. This pattern stands in stark contrast to classrooms in which criticism is socially unacceptable.

In 2014, Creative Leadership Solutions conducted interviews with successful young women, and we found what might be best described as "the good girl effect." A disturbing pattern emerged more than once in these interviews. They knew that the ideas of a classmate (as young as fourth grade) or a colleague (in prestigious consulting firms) were not very good. But these girls and young women had an astonishingly similar refrain: "I didn't want to hurt anyone's feelings." Their reluctance to express criticism not only hurt their own opportunities for career and academic advancement but also did no favors for their schools or employers. Reluctance to criticize and evaluate is the ally of mediocrity.

Avoid Assessment of Creativity

Grant Wiggins (2012) makes the case for assessing creativity in his seminal article, "On Assessing for Creativity: Yes You Can, and Yes You Should." He explains that we do students no favors by not assessing their creative work. Students know, Wiggins contends, the difference between boring stories and engaging stories. Their creative work improves with assessment and feedback. Therefore, the reluctance of parents, teachers, and fellow students to offer clear and honest feedback may create a false sense of self-esteem, but it diminishes creativity. This kind of professional practice discourages creativity as well as the attitudes and beliefs that lie beneath that practice.

Attitudes and Beliefs That Undermine Creativity

The professional practices described in the previous section spring from underlying attitudes and beliefs that undermine creativity. It's important to note that educators are very smart people who can hold two opposing ideas. They can believe fervently in the value of creativity and simultaneously hold beliefs that discourage creative development. There is absolutely no malice among people who hold these beliefs. People of goodwill and great intellect can hold beliefs contrary to the evidence. Nevertheless, if our ultimate goal is to improve the creative environment in schools, then we must objectively compare our beliefs to the evidence and, when the two diverge, go with the evidence.

Creativity Is a Natural Talent or Gift

Mozart, Maya Angelou, Michelangelo—it's obvious that these great creative geniuses were born with exceptional talent. In *Talent Is Overrated: What Really Separates World-Class Performers from Everybody Else*, Geoff Colvin (2008) makes the case that superior achievers, from chess champions to athletes to musicians to writers, succeed not merely because of natural talent or mysterious gifts but because they engage in deliberate practice. His observations are consistent with an interview I conducted in 2012 with two Boston Symphony Orchestra musicians, whose son, a French horn player, appeared to be a prodigy. His parents, who performed with one of the best orchestras in the world, insisted that their son's success was no more remarkable than their own. Isolate and repeat, they explained, was the secret to their son's success at a young age. He learned that the key to success was not waiting for the gift of the muse but what Colvin calls *deliberate practice.* One of the characteristics of practice is that it is not particularly fun. While the end result of hard work might be what Csikszentmihalyi (1996) calls *flow,* and actually supremely enjoyable, the process of getting to flow involves hard work. For the writer, it is penning many drafts, getting brutal feedback, editing, and rewriting. For the artist, including Michelangelo, da Vinci, Rodin, and Monet, it is not a process of immediate inspiration but of many canvases, drawings, molds, and almost completed works that were smashed and slashed. Creativity, in brief, is not the result of first drafts.

Real Creative Work Is Distinctly Original

One of the most piercing epithets that can be hurled in the academic world is that a work is derivative. This philosophy of elevating the truly original over the derivative is echoed in many of the K–12 creativity assessments that we reviewed in the *International Study of Creativity Rubrics.* There is just one problem—*everything is derivative.* I have learned from reviewing many doctoral dissertation prospectuses and book proposals that when the author claims that his or her work is completely original and no one has ever done it before, that is code for "I haven't completed my literature review" and "If anyone has done this, I haven't bothered to read it."

Two of the best visual illustrations of the progress of artistic work over time are the Picasso exhibit in the Hirshhorn Museum in Washington, D.C., and the world-class collection of impressionist works at the Musée d'Orsay in Paris. While we marvel at the invention of cubism, pointillism, and impressionism, it's important to note that none of these artistic breakthroughs are inventions at all.

As a careful observer at these museums will see, striking works of art are the result of a great deal of trial and error, observation of colleagues, and an untold number of destroyed drafts. What we see as great works of originality are, in fact, derivative—the result of years of trial and error, observations of peers, often brutal feedback, and commitment to a cycle of continuous improvement.

The same phenomenon can be observed in literature. We tend to study the great original works of the literary canon, and it is certainly a good idea to have exemplars to which we can compare our work. However, if we want students to understand the difficult journey from idea generation through multiple drafts to the final creative work, we would do well to have them study the failures of the great masters. Many of these failures are lost to history, with frustrated artists burning their early efforts that were the foundation of later masterpieces. But sometimes, we are fortunate enough to have a cache of work by great authors and artists. Samuel Clemens may have written some great novels, but he was also a hack who delivered dilettantish lectures to restore his bank account. Anne Frank's (1947) *The Diary of a Young Girl* contains deeply moving scenes and adolescent reflections, along with what some would consider uninteresting and pedantic prose. The key is that great work in any field does not exist in isolation, the result of mysterious original inspiration. Rather, great creative work is derivative, building on previous explorations of the creator, colleagues, and the world at large.

Academic literature about creativity has made much of "Big C, little c" as a false dichotomy, with the claim that the Big C represents breakthrough insights, while the little c is merely the application of others' creative work (Runco & Albert, 2010). Other writers have claimed that this also illustrates the difference between creativity and innovation, with the little c (small ideas that enrich our daily lives) only building on the Big C (rare breakthroughs). But the history of creativity leads to a strikingly different conclusion. Creativity depends on deep understanding of what came before. Picasso created a lot of representational art before he ventured into cubism. Rodin became an expert at drawing before he pursued sculpture. Musician John

Cage created the famous piece *4'33"*, which includes him sitting at a piano for almost five minutes of silence. It was a striking creative breakthrough for many music critics. But we would fail as responsible music lovers if we did not acknowledge that before his creative experimentation, Cage learned to play scales, chords, and arpeggios.

One of the key elements of assessing creativity is defining what creativity is. Prevailing definitions of creativity distinguish between creativity and innovation, with the creativity being original and the innovation being practical. Creativity is novel, while innovation is merely derivative. This distinction is popular, but it is popular nonsense. When we insist that students are creative only when they (and their teachers) acknowledge no precedent for their work, we are not encouraging creativity, we are encouraging intellectual laziness.

Creativity Cannot Happen Without Inspiration

One of the attitudes that most undermines creativity in the classroom is the myth of the muse. For at least three millennia, the prevailing explanation for creativity was divine inspiration. The Greeks called them the muses, a linguistic heritage that gives us the modern museum. African, Asian, Nordic, Celtic, Mayan, Persian, and American Indian civilizations shared the same tendency to attribute creative insights to divine inspiration. But while contemporary writers may no longer give tribute to the muse Calliope and her eight sisters, the myth of the muse casts a long shadow that, to this day, colors the way many people view artistic work. We may not attribute creative inspiration to the gods, but it remains tempting to think of creativity in quasi-mystical terms. In an essay for *The New-England* magazine, Victor Hugo (1835) writes, "It seems that poetic inspiration has in it something too sublime for the common nature of man" (p. 204). Even now in the 21st century, we still cling to the belief that creativity is a mysterious force bestowed on a special segment of the population at birth. The environment, the myth continues, can neither nurture nor crush these creative souls.

They have been known by many names: bards, bohemians, the tortured artist, the absentminded professor, or by talk-show radio hosts of a certain stripe, as "lazy bums." We all recognize the caricature: head aloft in the clouds or margin deep into a book, unconcerned with conventional appearance or custom. The *creative types* are simultaneously ridiculed for eccentricity and lauded for genius. They are a trope in fiction from Sherlock Holmes to Victor Frankenstein and routinely witnessed in the real world from the hipster communes of Brooklyn, New York, to the one black sheep at every family reunion. Regardless of the specifics, they are defined not only in their capacity to be creative but also for their opposition to the norm. It is a distinction played out over and over again: there are those who can create, and then there are the rest of us.

The U.S. Department of Labor even distinguishes between creative and noncreative professions (Burkus, 2014). But for the most part, this distinction is an artificial one. The notion that some people are simply born creative, that the miracle of invention can somehow be attributed to genes, was long ago undermined in a research study of fraternal and identical twins conducted in 1973. After testing more than one hundred pairs of twins, researchers found "little consistent or compelling evidence . . . to support the notion of a genetic component in creativity" (Reznikoff, Domino, Bridges, & Honeyman, 1973).

Left-Brain and Right-Brain Differences Heavily Influence Creativity

One must approach this intellectual territory with some trepidation. If you tell people that left-brain, right-brain dichotomies are irrelevant and an urban myth, you risk the same backlash as telling them that the learning styles theory may sound persuasive but is unsupported by the evidence. It certainly is true that different parts of the brain control different parts of the body, a phenomenon observed in stroke patients as well as those who have suffered brain injuries with a distinctive impact on speech and motor skills. However, the leap that creative people are left-brained and analytical people are right-brained has been correctly labeled a myth and a hoax (Wanjek, 2013). Even a casual observer of Leonardo da Vinci's work might suggest that artists are analytical and creative. The same is true of Nobel laureates in mathematics, science, physics, and literature. Perhaps this is the result of the zeal in some quarters to label students as gifted, exceptional, twice-exceptional, kinesthetic, auditory, visual, and so on. It is tragic loss of human potential when, on the flimsiest of evidence, children and adults are labeled with one dominant brain hemisphere or the other, and then encouraged to pursue their strengths.

Creative Inspiration Is Like Lightning

William Wordsworth expressed the view of generations of children and adults when he wrote, "My heart leaps up when I behold a rainbow in the sky" (Till, 1994, p. 90). There are sights in nature, great works of art, the curtain of a moving play, and the final note of a symphony, just to name a few potential sparks of creative inspiration. We can honor the power of these moments without concluding that, in the absence of this creative lightning, efforts at creativity are futile. Teachers can create opportunities for creativity routinely in classrooms, most particularly in how they express their expectations of students. Some ways of injecting creativity into an otherwise pedestrian moment in the classroom might include the following:

- Expressing an educated guess before conducting a Google or dictionary search

- Drawing a cause-and-effect diagram before each historical or scientific analysis

- Requiring plausible alternative answers to a question in geography, science, history, economics, or literature

Teachers can, in brief, create an environment that is conducive to creativity and need not wait for creative inspiration to strike.

The "Big C, little c" dichotomy described previously supports the belief that executing an idea isn't as important as generating the original insight, which is demonstrably false. Mark Runco (2014) argues that there is no evidence for this dichotomy. More importantly, the emphasis on Big C creativity undermines the essential work of little c, which is the foundation for applying and disseminating Big C ideas.

He argues:

> Little c creativity is meaningful in and of itself. This is
> in part because it is not really extricable from Big C
> creativity. Little c creativity may develop into Big C cre-
> ativity. Big C creativity involves things that lead to so-
> cial recognition, but the creativity results from the same
> process that is involved in little c creativity. (p. 132)

Standards of Evidence

As you reflect on these practices and attitudes, perhaps you find
some of them a bit strident but well within the realm of acceptabil-
ity. Perhaps you flatly disagree with some and strongly agree with
others. When we are confronted with vigorously argued assertions,
there is a spectrum of responses that we can offer.

Personal Beliefs

The first standard of evidence—and in my experience, the most
common—is personal beliefs. In matters of philosophy and reli-
gion, this is a perfectly reasonable standard of evidence, but it is
troubling when people of any age resort to personal beliefs in evaluating research propositions. For example, one might say, "I believe
that if we do not award zeros for missing work, then students will
become lazy, undisciplined, and refuse to turn in homework." This
is a reasonable statement of belief, but it is not an accurate conclusion based on the best available evidence (Guskey, 2014). Beliefs,
however strongly held, are not a substitute for evidence.

Personal Experience

The second standard of evidence is personal experience. It may be
the case that in the experience of an individual practitioner, creativity is the result of inspiration and not the result of multiple instances
of trial and error. Personal experience can be accurate in the particu-
lars but inaccurate in the generalities. For example, Lutherans may
be better singers than Methodists in the experience of one auditor,
but that's a relatively low standard of evidence and, to put it mildly,

dependent on a fairly selective sample size. I know of atheists who sing lustily in the Kings College Choir with tone and enthusiasm sufficient to exceed other congregations I have heard, but to generalize such a person impugns Protestants, atheists, the University of Cambridge, and all of the choristers omitted in this illustration. Personal experience, particularly in the domain of creativity, is interesting but hardly generalizable.

Collective Experience

The third standard of evidence is collective experience. For example, one might say, "It's not just me but the collective observations of my colleagues that lead me to conclude that brainstorming, unfettered by criticism, is the best way to generate creative ideas." This may well be true, as advertising executives initiated this pattern of brainstorming in the 1940s. For more than half a century, it remained unchallenged as the most effective way for groups to generate new and creative ideas. When an idea is accepted enthusiastically and uncritically, without comparison to alternatives, the hypothesis that the idea works is difficult to avoid and very likely to be confirmed by group expectations. But groupthink (Janis, 1982) is a dangerous illusion, one in which the confirmation of one's expectations by colleagues can lead to disastrous consequences. In the context of school, groupthink can lead to bullying, stereotyping, and generalizations about race, gender, accent, and appearance, all justified by the validation of collective experience. The experiences of teachers who examine their own work in the classroom need not be haphazard. Systematic collective observations, such as those in the best PLCs, can have a powerfully energizing effect on the improvement of professional practices (DuFour & Fullan, 2014).

Systematic Observation

The fourth standard of evidence is systematic observation. For example, imagine that you have twelve elementary schools in your school district. Six schools were randomly assigned to continue the current homework policy, which requires teachers to mark as a failure each incomplete homework submission. The remaining six schools applied an alternative homework policy that requires teachers to provide alternative times during the school day to complete the homework. The results of this experiment concluded that 92 percent of the students in the second group completed homework, while 48 percent of students in the first group completed homework. In addition, more than 80 percent of students in the second group scored a B or higher on their next report card, while fewer than 20 percent of students in the first group did so.

Surely these observations are limited. They only include twelve schools and about five thousand students. But the quality of the methodology and the quantity of observations surely exceed the first three standards of evidence—personal beliefs, personal experience, and collective experience.

Preponderance of Evidence

The fifth and final standard of evidence is the preponderance of evidence. This includes different methods, different researchers, and different contexts, all addressing the same issue. Consider, for example, different perspectives on the impact of effective feedback on student learning. Ken O'Connor (2009) provides compelling case studies regarding the impact of accurate feedback on student learning. Thomas Guskey (2014) provides a collection of evidence from a variety of observational, experimental, and quasi-experimental designs. Robert Marzano (2007) offers a synthesis of studies to support his conclusions for formative assessments and standards-based grading, and John Hattie and Gregory Yates (2014) provide a synthesis of meta-analyses with remarkably similar conclusions about the value and impact of clear, specific, and frequent feedback. Educators who have considered all of these sources and more are prepared to say, "Based on the preponderance of evidence, we have concluded that this particular grading and reporting strategy is effective and has earned our professional confidence."

There is an antidote to the cultures, practices, and attitudes that undermine creativity, and that is the subject of the next chapter.

Chapter 4

How Educators and Leaders Can Encourage Creativity

As the evidence in chapter 1 makes clear, creativity is essential for students, workers, educators, and leaders not only in the creative arts but also in every domain, including education, business, health care, technology, and the nonprofit world. The primary challenge is how to transform our creative aspirations into practical actions. In chapter 3, we suggested practices and attitudes to be avoided. Now we come to powerful practices that *encourage* creativity. One of the most powerful practices that teachers and leaders can implement to promote creativity is providing feedback that is timely, accurate, and specific (Hattie, 2012; Hattie & Yates, 2014). This chapter offers a systematic way in which to offer this feedback, not only during classroom activities explicitly described to engender creativity but also during almost *all* activities. When feedback improves, student performance improves, which not only leads to improved creativity but also improved academic performance across the board. We have identified eight dimensions for providing effective feedback through creativity assessment.

Eight Dimensions of Creativity Assessment

The eight dimensions of creativity assessment were developed as a result of extensive research into what sorts of teacher feedback and assessments were most likely to encourage creativity. Some of these dimensions might appear obvious—who wouldn't want a research basis for his or her assessments? However, there is more here than meets the eye. For example, although it is widely discredited, unfiltered brainstorming is a common requirement of creativity assessments. Similarly, most people would agree that providing source material for a project is a good idea, but many classroom assessments actively discourage source material by requiring students to submit work that is entirely novel and original. Citing sources, in the context of those assessments, would relegate student work as derivative rather than original.

1. **Research basis:** This is the extent to which students and teachers understand the research processes that support and hinder creativity.

2. **Multidisciplinary perspective:** This is the degree to which student work includes different perspectives from different worlds of academic thought.

3. **Source material:** Creative artists honor the shoulders on which they stand. Leibniz and Newton developed calculus by acknowledging the mathematical work of their predecessors. The notes from the lyre, cymbals, drum, and human voice formed the musical basis for compositions in antiquity. The Renaissance gave us progressively more complex keyboards and musical notations. From ancient to relatively recent times, these formed the building blocks not only for the work of Bach, Beethoven, and Brahms but also for the anonymous Gregorian monks who preserved medieval harmonies, the Pythagoreans who developed original

rules for the perfect intervals among tones, and great contemporary jazz and classical artists of the 21st century. Great writers are great readers; great artists are great observers; and great musicians are great listeners, whether they listen to silence, the sounds of nature, or the echoes of their compositional predecessors. This is why creativity rubrics and definitions of the term *creativity* are incorrect when they insist that real creativity is completely novel and original.

4. **Clarity of guidelines:** Every assessment must be reliable; that is, it provides consistent feedback to the student, even when different evaluators consider the students' work. In the context of performance assessments, one of the greatest indicators of consistency and reliability is the specificity of performance descriptions. This requirement for clarity is essential, whether teachers are providing on-the-spot feedback in the classroom, using rubrics for a performance assessment, or receiving feedback from an administrator. Without clarity, the recipient of feedback cannot improve.

5. **Product:** Every creative enterprise should produce a product—perhaps a mathematical formula, a scientific experiment, an analysis of historical documents, a painting, a musical composition, a character sketch, or a journal article. Each of these and many more can reflect the creativity of the student, but it's not enough for students to point to their head and proudly say, "It's all in there."

6. **Process:** If we expect creativity to have social value, then the process of developing creative products must be documented and shared. However magical and mystical the process may seem to outsiders, we

should insist that students help the world understand the process behind their work. J. K. Rowling had an elaborate chart with characters, plots, and relationships for all of the *Harry Potter* characters. Einstein wrote furious notes while rocking his baby at night and working at the Swiss patent office by day. Galileo documented thousands of observations, which, he thought, would support his theories. Sometimes he was right and sometimes not. That is precisely the value of the documenting process. When teachers experience a gain in achievement or a surge of creativity in the classroom, it is imperative that they explain to their colleagues the context of those changes, including the influence of their professional practices on student results.

7. **Collaboration:** If teachers expect students to collaborate, then they must assess the process and personal commitment each student invests in the collaborative effort. This is very tricky, as many students feel frustrated when their work is held hostage to a classmate.

8. **Practice and error:** There is no creativity without error. Assessments that require a beautiful product, but do not also expect to see several less beautiful products along the way, give students the false impression that creativity is born of one-shot efforts by clever students who are bright enough to get it right the first time. Hardly any assessment or feedback could cause greater damage to the creative enterprise. The requirement for a cycle of practice, error, feedback, and improvement happens every day in excellent music and athletics classes, but the impulse in many other classes is to get it right the first time. The homework assignment that

has all items completed correctly is lauded far more frequently than the homework assignment that has a note from the student saying, "What I learned from today's homework: here is what I know, here is what I think I know, and here is what I don't know."

These eight dimensions can be a bit overwhelming, so let us first consider the current state of creativity assessment. Before you are too harsh on yourself (remember the Goldilocks Principle—feedback that is accurate but not brutally paralyzing), consider the results from the *International Study of Creativity Rubrics* conducted by Creative Leadership Solutions in 2014 and published here for the first time.

The Current State of Creativity Assessment

The good news is that more teachers and school leaders are taking creativity seriously, and many are endeavoring to assess it. For teachers who are willing to share their work with colleagues and researchers, we are extremely grateful. The purpose of the following section is not to level criticism but rather to practice what we preach—use the process of experimentation, error, and learning in order to improve the quality of creativity assessment. In the *International Study of Creativity Rubrics*, we reviewed more than one hundred creativity rubrics, including K–12, elementary, secondary, and college, and evaluated them on the eight dimensions of creativity assessment. We created a metarubric—a "rubric for rubrics"—to give us an objective assessment of the quality of each rubric. For each dimension, we considered four levels of performance, each of which is described in the following text. In testing the reliability of the metarubric, we found a greater than 90 percent consistency between two independent raters. Each rubric was rated on the eight dimensions, and each dimension was assessed on a four-point scale, yielding more than eight hundred data points for consideration. Because of the four-point scale and eight dimensions, the maximum possible score for any individual rubric was 32. We set standards very high at the exemplary level but also at the proficient level. Therefore, any rubric that scored between 25 and 32 was designated as *exemplary*. Rubrics that scored from 17 to 24 were labeled *proficient*. Rubrics that scored 9 to 16 were called *progressing*; and rubrics that scored from 1 to 8 (meaning that at best they were the lowest rating, and in some cases, a zero rating in several dimensions) were called *developing*.

It is important to note that these selections were not random and do not represent the universe of rubrics teachers use. In fact, this sample, based on voluntary submissions by educators who believe that their work should be shared and emulated, represents a far superior level of rubric performance than if we accessed a random sample of rubrics from around the United States. For those teachers willing to share their work, we applaud that professionalism and generosity. Therefore, the following notes are not intended as mean-spirited criticism but rather as the professional feedback on which both students and professionals depend in order to improve. In our assessment, we found the following.

- Of the elementary rubrics, 29 percent were progressing, and 71 percent were proficient. We found no elementary rubrics that met the standard for exemplary, and none were labeled as developing.

- Of the secondary rubrics, 6 percent were exemplary, 53 percent were progressing, and 41 percent were proficient.

- Of the K–12 rubrics, 73 percent were proficient, 20 percent were progressing, and 7 percent were exemplary.

Although the absence of rubrics with the lowest composite scores indicates that creativity rubrics are often on the right track, the scarcity of the highest composite scores suggests that we have a long way to go to significantly improve the quality of creativity rubrics.

The data suggest that the strongest dimensions in current teacher assessment of creativity, at least in terms of the availability of rubrics earning a top score of 4, are multidisciplinary perspective and clarity of guidelines. The weakest dimensions are product, collaboration, and practice and error, dimensions in which none of the rubrics in the sample earned a top rating. To be clear, we are not suggesting that this is a representative sample of all creativity rubrics. In fact, it is a positively biased sample, because we only considered creativity rubrics that teachers and administrators were willing to share voluntarily. If you apply the same analysis to all creativity rubrics in your school, don't be surprised if your initial results are a bit lower. However, the prospect of lower assessment scores should not result in a failure to assess. This is the same mistake that students make when, confident that they can play the C-major scale, never attempt more difficult music. Too much professional development is a saccharine effort in affirmation rather than a challenge to improve professional performance on a continuous basis. When I hear people leave a staff development program saying, "That pretty much tells me that everything I've been doing is right," then I know that both the participants and the staff developer have wasted their time.

In the study, we analyzed rubrics that included K–12, elementary, secondary, and college. In terms of overall quality, we found that the K–12, secondary, and college rubrics were somewhat stronger than the elementary rubrics, and all of them needed work, particularly in adhering to research, encouraging collaboration, and requiring experimentation and evaluation.

Considering all rubrics in the sample, following are the percentages of rubrics that scored at the proficient or exemplary levels on each of the eight dimensions of creativity assessment.

1. **Research basis:** 42 percent
2. **Multidisciplinary perspective:** 49 percent

3. **Source material:** 34 percent

4. **Clarity of guidelines:** 52 percent

5. **Product:** 17 percent

6. **Process:** 41 percent

7. **Collaboration:** 9 percent

8. **Practice and error:** 20 percent

One of the most frequent challenges in translating research into action is persuading professionals of the relevance of research from other locations to their own school. The following section provides you with the opportunity to use the same metarubric that we used in the *International Study of Creativity Rubrics* and apply it to one of your own rubrics. You might select a rubric specifically designed to encourage creativity, or you could select any performance assessment rubric or scoring guide. If you prefer not to start with one of your own, you can visit **go.solution-tree.com/technology** to download the composite rubrics. Please note that these composite rubrics are not presented as exemplars but rather as fairly typical rubrics, with strengths and weaknesses, which allow you to apply the metarubric in a rigorous and thoughtful manner.

The composite rubrics are not the creation of any individual teacher or school but rather a synthesis of the more than one hundred rubrics that we evaluated. We recommend that you ask your colleagues to first work entirely alone, applying the metarubric to each of the sample creativity rubrics. Then, before comparing notes or debating the different ratings, simply tabulate the results, showing the percentage of participants in your group who rated each creativity assessment as a 1, 2, 3, or 4 for each dimension. Visit **go.solution-tree.com/technology** for a reproducible version of the "Metarubric for Assessing Creativity Rubrics" (pages 44–46), which you can use to assess the composite rubrics.

Metarubric for Assessing Creativity Rubrics

A good metarubric can only go so far in promoting effective creativity assessment. Without strong levels of agreement (we recommend 80 percent or more agreement when teachers independently score work), even the best rubric sends mixed messages to teachers and students, as it is unclear what they must do in order to improve. When these disagreements happen, and they *always* do, the conclusion must include the following mantra: the enemy is not one another; the enemy is ambiguity. In other words, blame us! If our creativity metarubric does not allow you to come to a consensus in which 80 percent or more of the faculty agrees on the rating, then the problem has nothing to do with the intellect or professionalism of the faculty but rather the problem is the ambiguity of the metarubric. When you recognize this, you can work together to improve the metarubric, rejecting our phrases and replacing them with words and phrases that allow you and your colleagues to come to an effective consensus. Our goal is not for you to implement our metarubric in your school but rather for you to own, implement, and use *your work and the work of your colleagues.*

The metarubric in figure 4.1 (pages 44–46) shows the eight dimensions of creativity assessment. These dimensions are not intended to evaluate or diminish the well-crafted assessment rubrics teachers have created but rather to serve as a platform for continuous improvement. Before you apply this metarubric to your own rubric or to those of colleagues, please consider applying the metarubric to the composite rubrics online. My experience is that teachers and students alike give much more consistent and useful feedback when they do not know the authors of the work. In addition, teachers become faster and more consistent in providing feedback when they have practiced using the metarubric with two or three anonymous rubrics before they attempt to use the metarubric with the actual work of colleagues.

Dimension	1–Developing	2–Progressing	3–Proficient	4–Exemplary
Research Basis	The rubric is based on intuition or hunches and has little basis in research, as evidenced by the promotion of practices that are contrary to research. For example, the rubric might encourage brainstorming without filtering or criticism.	The rubric includes some elements based in research and some other elements that are speculative, outdated, or not based on research.	The rubric reflects current research on the relationship between student actions and creative results.	The rubric reflects the latest and best research, including clear citations that other teachers, parents, or students can use to better understand the rubric writer's reasoning.
Multi-disciplinary Perspective	The rubric focuses narrowly on subjects and ideas within a single discipline, and explicitly punishes or dissuades students from using sources or media from other disciplines.	The rubric allows students to explore projects using an individualized, interdisciplinary approach, but does not clearly promote that approach.	The rubric specifically encourages and rewards an interdisciplinary perspective.	The rubric encourages students to expand the scope of their work, through an iterative process, to include ideas and perspectives from three or more different disciplines and sources.
Source Material	The rubric expects students to be completely original and punishes the use of outside material for inspiration or use.	The rubric allows students to consider outside sources but makes no special note of the process.	The rubric encourages the use of a variety of digital, print, and personal sources to form the basis of the creative product for the current project.	The rubric requires the use of external sources and the identification of ideas from other sources on which the current project is based.

Dimension	1–Developing	2–Progressing	3–Proficient	4–Exemplary
Clarity of Guidelines	The rubric contains ambiguous language, which makes the difference between rubric levels unclear to students and inconsistently applied by teachers.	The rubric is expressed in language that is inaccessible to students. It may be clear to the teacher, but the obscurity and complexity of the language make the rubric of little use as a feedback tool.	The rubric guidelines clearly specify the criteria and performance levels by which the students are evaluated. The teacher has evidence that at least two different evaluators have used the rubric to come to very similar conclusions about student performance.	The rubric is clear and specific in how it distinguishes each performance level. A group of teachers, including those from different grade levels and from outside the subject discipline, applied the rubric to an anonymous piece of student work and came to very similar conclusions.
Product	The rubric calls for the creation of a work product, but the requirements are ambiguous or absent, and differences among performance levels are unclear. The teacher values process to the exclusion of product.	The rubric requires the creation of a work product, but there is no objective feedback that leads to improved product development through the submission of multiple drafts.	The rubric requires the teacher to objectively evaluate the student's work product using a clear assessment rubric.	The rubric requires the teacher to objectively evaluate the student's work product using a clear assessment rubric. There is evidence that students can, independently and in groups, use the rubric to revise and improve the product.

Figure 4.1: Metarubric for assessing creativity rubrics.

Continued ↓

Dimension	1–Developing	2–Progressing	3–Proficient	4–Exemplary
Process	The rubric's process requirements are ambiguous, and differences among performance levels are not clear.	The rubric's process requirements are inconsistent, and students have difficulty using the rubric to improve their work.	The rubric has clear process requirements, and students can differentiate performance levels based on the rubric.	The rubric not only evaluates the end product but also student work through every step of the process. As a result of this feedback, there is evidence that students are improving their methods, processes, and products.
Collaboration	The rubric requires students to work in complete isolation, without the aid or feedback of other students or teachers. Getting hints, suggestions, or ideas from other students is strictly forbidden.	The rubric allows for collaborative or group work, but it includes no guidelines for evaluating the process of collaboration.	The rubric requires a portion of the project to be group based. It establishes clear guidelines as to how group collaboration works and how students share responsibilities for the process and product.	The rubric establishes guidelines for collaboration, including specifying which elements of the team product are the work of individual students, the work of two or three students, and the work of the entire team. It is clear from the rubric that great performance is a combination of work by individuals, pairs, and larger teams.
Practice and Error	The rubric promotes one-thought attempts at performance. The ideal submission is error free and done right the first time it is submitted to the teacher.	The rubric allows for redrafting work products that are not acceptable on the first attempt.	The rubric requires multiple drafts of work products, with students using the rubric to improve performance.	The rubric requires multiple drafts, and there is clear evidence that students learn from their mistakes. The ideal work is never error free but full of learning that results from a virtuous cycle of error, feedback, reflection, and improvement.

Scoring creativity rubrics with this metarubric is intellectually challenging and professionally rewarding. The best process for applying the metarubric is as follows.

1. Ask teachers to work alone, applying the metarubric to either one of their own rubrics or a composite rubric online (visit **go.solution-tree.com/technology**).

2. Identify areas of agreement and disagreement. The objective is not perfect agreement but an 80 percent or higher level of agreement. If five teachers collaborate on using the metarubric, then four out of five of them should agree about the specific score.

3. Consider the reasons for any sources of disagreement. Remember, the enemy is never one another. The enemy is ambiguity. Therefore, feel free to revise the language of the metarubric until it provides the clarity necessary for your group to achieve at least 80 percent agreement.

4. Repeat this process with at least two additional rubrics. Too often in professional development activities, participants complete a task once and shelve it, finding it too easy and, therefore, irrelevant. Or, they find it too difficult and, therefore, tiresome and overwhelming. But when the metarubric is applied three or more times, two interesting phenomena occur. First, teachers apply the metarubric considerably faster. Second, the level of faculty agreement gets considerably higher. This is identical to observations made in the past about teachers getting faster and more consistent the more frequently they practice applying rubrics to student work (Reeves, 2006).

As you gain confidence in applying the metarubric in this chapter, you may want to apply it in a group session with brave colleagues who are willing to have their own rubrics assessed and improved. Until then, consider using the composite rubrics online for practice.

Chapter 5

Adapting the Four Essential Questions of PLCs to Creativity

The relationship between creativity and achievement is very strong, a conclusion reached not only by Hattie but also by Professor Kyung Hee Kim of the College of William and Mary. In a landmark study, including more than three hundred thousand students over twenty years, Kim (2011) finds that creativity is declining among American students, particularly with regard to the creative skills of students in kindergarten through third grade. The period under study, 1990 to 2008, coincides with a stagnation or decline, depending on the data selected, in student achievement. While putative IQ scores have risen, achievement—at least as measured in local, state, and international assessments—has withered. Hattie (2012) finds that school programs designed to enhance creativity are associated with improved achievement results.

However, statistical relationships can be tricky to interpret, as we will discuss later in this chapter. Those who conclude that creativity is not a gift of the muses but available to virtually any student—a conclusion strongly reinforced by the research we reviewed on the subject—find that the work of Kim and Hattie reinforces our previous conclusions. Just as effective literacy and mathematics programs can improve results for *all* students, including those who have been underperforming, so can professional practices that encourage creativity, such as those described in chapter 4. But opponents of the "all students can learn" hypothesis may look at the same data and come to a different conclusion: clever students are creative, and creative students are clever—who is to say which is the education chicken and which is the performance egg?

Gardner (1993) expresses it best when he acknowledges the undeniable power of genius, but he also notes that Picasso, for example, was mediocre in his early years as an artist and, like da Vinci and Michelangelo, discarded many works that prevent an objective evaluation of the totality of his work. Every great creative breakthrough in science, the arts, literature, and politics (Gardner examines the career of Gandhi) has been accompanied by exceptional amounts of work, trial, error, feedback, rejection, and ultimately, vindication and success. It is a lot easier to recognize genius through the rearview mirror of history than it is to recognize it during a spectacular failure. Therefore, while it may be a stretch to say creativity can be, as it were, created, it is certainly true that schools can create environments that either encourage or discourage creativity.

A generation ago, skeptics might have claimed that advanced mathematics can't be taught, particularly after mathematical abilities were established in the early grades. But data on mathematics achievement strongly suggest that even students who underperformed in mathematics in the past can excel in advanced courses in statistics and calculus (Kanold, 2012). Every research claim is subject to error. The acknowledgment of error is central to research. Errors are categorized in two ways—(1) the probability that a true hypothesis is rejected and (2) the probability that a false hypothesis is accepted. When it comes to creativity and student achievement, the options do not include an error-free zone. Rather, we must choose wisely the errors we are willing to make. Based on the evidence in this book, the better error to make is one in which we attempt to enhance creativity and student achievement by risking failure rather than failing to make the attempt and forego success.

PLCs and Achievement

The impact of PLCs on student achievement is significant and sustained—that is, if, and it's a *big if*, PLCs are implemented deeply, well, and over a long period of time. In 2014, Creative Leadership Solutions conducted an analysis of a specific subset of PLC schools—those using the PLC model developed by Richard DuFour, Rebecca DuFour, Robert Eaker, and Thomas Many (2006). We found substantial relationships between PLC implementation and student achievement. This sample included 196 schools from the United States, Canada, Australia, and Singapore and more than 750,000 students. The world of statistical relationships is treacherous, so it is important to be careful in any interpretation of data that shows one variable relating to another. We cannot claim definitively that cigarette smoking *always* causes cancer, as my maternal grandfather smoked, even after he was reduced to one lung, and lived vigorously into his nineties. My paternal grandmother smoked a corncob pipe and also lived a long life. This is not a recommendation for smoking or an excuse for any other questionable health habits that are statistically related to cancer but rather an acknowledgment of the limits of statistical relationships.

When it comes to student achievement, there are strong relationships between some (but not very many) instructional interventions and student achievement. Because the studies, sample sizes, and sample sources are so compelling, it's tempting to claim, for example, that requiring more nonfiction writing causes improved student achievement in science, mathematics, social studies, and reading. Similarly, the research on effective teacher feedback suggests that feedback is so strongly associated with improved student achievement that it causes better results. But any time one claims a statistical relationship, critics quickly cry, "Correlation is not causation!" They are correct. The more modest claim is not that writing *causes* higher achievement but rather that the hypothesis of "we don't have time for writing—we have to study for the test" is certainly untrue. The data show that when more time is devoted to writing, students achieve at higher levels.

Similarly, the claim that "we don't have time for more frequent and detailed feedback—we have to prepare to the test" is also untrue, as classrooms, schools, and districts that engage in effective feedback have better results. It's not necessary to claim causality to argue in favor of a professional practice. However, it's important to be modest about the other potential causes of achievement, such as student socioeconomic status. Certainly, socioeconomic status is important—but so are teachers and education leaders. A wise strategy for every education professional is to acknowledge the variables we cannot control but to focus on the variables we can control. So it is in the spirit of recognizing these complexities, and the necessity for modest claims, that we offer the following evidence from more than 750,000 students in four countries.

First, when considering both the implementation model (the use of PLCs) and the duration of implementation (number of years), PLCs have a significant relationship to gains in student achievement. For example, school gains in mathematics for those implementing PLCs over eight years are five times as great as for those implementing PLCs for only three years (R^2, the amount of variation in achievement, explains the variation in duration of PLC implementation, .62). The numbers for English language arts are similarly compelling ($R^2 = .57$). The relationship for science is even greater ($R^2 = .76$). Remember, this does not mean that PLCs *caused* gains in student achievement. It does, however, definitively undermine the often-heard claim that "we don't have time for PLCs, because we need to spend more time preparing for tests." If that were true, then these statistical relationships should be nearly zero or, when expressed as a simple correlation coefficient, negative. In this example of the duration of PLCs and student achievement, the graphs show a positive correlation—simply put, the longer that schools persist in implementing PLCs, the greater the gains in student achievement.

Numbers alone, however, do not tell the complete story of any inquiry. There is a story behind the numbers, in which qualitative inquiry can provide insight into the conditions underlying the statistical relationships. In the case of the 196 schools in this study, the testimony from schools engaging in PLCs for more than five years is significantly different from those who are relatively early into their journey. The good news is that there is a confluence between quantitative and qualitative research—seeing statistics through the lens of personal stories. The bad news is that five years is an eternity for most education reforms. While some give lip service to the value of focus and persistence, the reality is that leadership turnover and short funding cycles often mean that even the most successful initiatives are doomed to be replaced or crowded out within three years after initiation. Having confidence in the relationship between PLCs and achievement, and between achievement and creativity, is a good start. The more difficult challenge is translating these research findings into practical action steps in classrooms and schools.

Using the Four Essential Questions to Enhance Creativity and Achievement

At the heart of effective PLC implementation are the four essential questions. They are:

1. What is it we want our students to learn?

2. How will we know if each student has learned it?

3. How will we respond when some students do not learn it?

4. How can we extend and enrich the learning for
    students who have demonstrated proficiency?
    (DuFour et al., 2006, p. 91)

In the context of establishing a culture that nurtures and encourages creativity, it is essential that faculty and administrators have clarity about the four essential questions. We must think not only in terms of what we want students to learn but also what we want teachers and administrators to learn and be able to do. Consider placing the four essential questions in the context of creativity.

1. What is it we want our students (and teachers and administrators) to learn?

    • Mistakes are necessary and valuable.

    • Rugged individualism is nice, but collaboration is more effective.

    • Collaborating with colleagues is neither cheating (for students) nor professionally risky (for teachers who are working in a competitive evaluation system).

    • Your first draft (for example, a drawing in primary school or a dissertation in graduate school) is never your last draft.

    • If we expect students and colleagues to improve, we must provide clear guidance not only for the performance we expect, but also for incremental feedback on how to get to the next level of learning.

    • Pythagoras was both a mathematician and musician. Physicists can be poets. Teachers in government and economics can sing, however off-key, the songs of rebellion that characterize great movements in history. In brief, we want students, teachers, and leaders to respect every discipline and create regular opportunities to integrate them.

- Beliefs are important but not as important as evidence.

- Students and faculty should be ready to challenge, politely but insistently, the difference between statements of belief and statements of evidence. In education, as in science, many ideas and concepts are in doubt, but there is also a confluence of opinion on some bedrock principles. Teaching both sides of the feedback controversy, most commonly expressed in bizarre grading policies, is like teaching both sides of the gravity question.

2. How will we know if each student has learned it?

We assess what we value. If the only items that we assess and report are standardized test scores, then don't expect a renaissance of creativity. We can and must assess creativity and, of equal importance, the manner in which creativity is taught and assessed. We must confront the divergence between our values and practices. Virtually every school claims to value a growing number of 21st century skills. However, it is not logical for an education system to claim in its mission and vision statements that it values these skills, foremost among them creativity and collaboration, and then omit creativity and punish collaboration. One local university was shocked to learn that students who attended the same study group provided the same answers on an exam. The ensuing allegations of academic dishonesty ensure that next year's crop of undergraduates will not make the same mistake. They may or may not cheat, but they certainly will not collaborate.

3. How will we respond when some students (and adults) do not learn it?

    We must abandon the ethic of getting it right the first time and replace it with commitment to a process of honest acknowledgment of error, acceptance of feedback, and incremental improvement. In an environment in which an A is the only acceptable grade for students and teachers (whose livelihoods may depend on toxic evaluation systems), critical feedback might be difficult. When feedback has evaluative consequences for students, the teacher's honest but critical feedback might possibly lead to a challenge of the teacher's professional judgment or even threats of litigation. Therefore, we must distinguish clearly between feedback and evaluation. Evaluation can be threatening and create an adversarial environment. Feedback, when done well (fair, accurate, specific, and timely) can improve performance by everyone in the education system.

    Despite the multibillion-dollar commitments schools have made to technology, including student grading and teacher observation systems, the best response when some students and adults do not learn what we expect is not a negative entry into the database but rather informal feedback that is clearly not an evaluation, grade, or formal observation (Reeves, 2011).

4. How can we extend and enrich the learning for students who have demonstrated proficiency?

    There is great danger in extending creative learning opportunities only to students and teachers who are already masters of their subjects. Rather than offering creative opportunities only after achievement and success in academic disciplines, we should instead heed Gardner's (2009) advice that disciplinary excellence and creativity are intertwined. For those students who have demonstrated proficiency, a focus on creativity provides an evergreen source of challenge, inspiration, and intrinsic motivation. High-performing students are apt to become quickly bored and disenchanted. But the elements of creativity can always be improved; indeed, it is a lifelong opportunity for stimulation and personal challenge. Monet painted great works half a century after the successful Paris exhibition in which he challenged, at great risk, the prevailing orthodoxy of the art world. Elliott Carter conducted great orchestras into his nineties and composed great symphonic works after his centenary.

Schools often stifle creativity as students move from elementary into secondary school on the pretense that students must become ready for the real world of work, as in a 19th century factory, on schedule and to specification. Two centuries later, the language of the factory pervades discussions of student assessment. Committing to a creative environment, not just for students who have achieved academic proficiency but *all* students, offers an opportunity to break free of the Industrial Revolution and join the Creative Revolution.

Chapter 6

Creativity for Education Policymakers

We cannot expect creativity in the classroom if we do not see it in the boardroom, state legislative chambers, or the halls of Congress. The following are five practices policymakers can implement to keep creativity alive in education.

1. Inclusion
2. Collaboration
3. Debate, dissent, and discipline in decision making
4. Accountability
5. Forgiveness

The 21st century has seen the enormous influence of state and national policymakers on the classroom. In the early 1990s, a dozen states replaced self-defined standards of success by local school districts with statewide standards, backed up with state-mandated assessments. This coincided with the beginning of the decline in student creativity explored by Kim (2011). Shortly after the inauguration of President George W. Bush in January of 2001, a majority of both houses of Congress passed with bipartisan support the No Child Left Behind Act. This was the first legislative action of the new administration. It required that every state establish academic content standards and grade-level assessments to determine the degree to which each state was making progress toward 100 percent proficiency thirteen years hence. The logic was that the kindergarten students of 2001, with the benefit of the No Child Left Behind Act, would be motivated, from a combination of threats and incentives, to achieve universal proficiency. Eight years of No Child Left Behind were followed by Race to the Top, an effort to do with administrative mandates and federal economic incentives what the previous years of legislative mandates could not do. After many years of experimentation in education policy, we know one thing for certain: threats, mandates, bribes, and coercion accomplish compliance and even a degree of creativity, even if the highest and best use of that term is evasion and defiance.

Now in the 21st century, political leaders of every stripe should be chastened by the gap between the aspirations of policymakers and the realities of the classroom. Every politician since George Washington has expressed frustration with Congress, and today's residents of Capitol Hill have no exclusive claim on low popularity. The musical *The Music Man* famously ridiculed the local school board, represented as a contentious barbershop quartet. However, contempt and ridicule are rarely effective strategies for creating bold and imaginative policies. What is a discouraged policymaker to do? We offer the following five suggestions to help policymakers escape from the mire of despair to the promise, if not the assurance, of a creative future.

Inclusion

School-board members, legislators, and members of Congress are most likely frustrated by the endless line of witnesses who demand to be heard, whether it is posing before the cameras of local cable television—surely the dinosaur of 21st century media—or seven-figure-salary lobbyists advancing their interests at the state and national levels. The antidote to this tedium is not denying a forum to citizens who have a right to express themselves but rather including those who have no axe to grind nor private interest to represent. When reviewing a list of witnesses who wish to appear before a local school board or legislative/congressional committee, policymakers should ask, "Who's missing?" Politicians reflexively balance school administrators with union leaders, but they should also consider asking creativity advocates from within and outside of the education system to join the debate. The term *creativity advocates* is not only limited to those associated with the creative arts but also those willing to challenge prevailing systems of evaluation, assessment, and accountability that undermine creativity. Creativity advocates are not always obvious, but one characteristic that clearly identifies them is their willingness to engage in divergent thinking. While most policymakers seek harmony and agreement, they would be wise to consider that the absence of contention in the boardroom or hearing room means only the *concealment* of contention. When everyone agrees on a proposal, policymakers should deliberately seek to find an advocate of alternatives. Although the original consensus may prevail, it makes for a better policymaking environment when proposals are accompanied by vigorous discussion and debate, not silent assent.

Collaboration

In the context of local school boards, open meeting laws are typically openly hostile to effective collaboration. Even a "reply all" email from one board member to colleagues can be deemed a violation of the law (Wisconsin Department of Justice, 2010). The prevailing context, in which the fear of litigation overshadows legitimate communication and collaboration, does not prevent effective collaboration among policymakers. Rather, it requires a context of collaboration in the sunshine rather than behind closed doors. Public collaboration by policymakers and leaders can set the right tone for every school. Collaborative inquiry is the opposite of posing for the cameras and requires thoughtful questions such as, "I haven't heard that point of view before; could you tell me more?" or "I'm pretty sure that I agree with you, but could you tell me why we both might be wrong?" Collaboration does not mean congeniality but rather using the strengths born of divergent thinking to create unexpected policy alternatives and better leadership choices.

Debate, Dissent, and Discipline in Decision Making

Dartmouth professor Sydney Finkelstein (2009, 2014) writes persuasively about why smart people make bad decisions. People do not rise to the heights of their professions in business, education, government, or the nonprofit world by being willfully ignorant and indolent. It takes real effort for such well-educated and hard-working leaders to make bad decisions. These leaders expend too much energy seeking consensus and too little demanding divergent thinking, the heart of creative leadership. They rejoice at unanimous votes and compliant colleagues, and demand buy-in, when deep inside they know that the arguments that don't happen in the boardroom occur in the parking lot. A better path is to welcome—in fact, demand—vigorous debate, dissent, and discipline in decision making. If everyone in the room agrees with the leader, then all but one of them are unnecessary. Comity is a wonderful attribute for a policymaking body but only when it occurs after, not before, a vigorous debate of alternatives. This only happens when staff members have the courage, backed by senior leadership, to provide alternatives and advocate for them.

Accountability

Perhaps the greatest impact policymakers can have on promoting a creative environment is the demand for accountability. If the mission, vision, and strategies give lip service to creativity, but their accountability system relies solely on test scores, then it is a formula for cynicism and hypocrisy. There is no contradiction between local, state, and national policymakers requiring schools to report annually on student achievement in reading and writing and the ability of local leaders to show their stakeholders all the other student and school activities through a public accountability report. An appropriate response by the local system should be, "We do not avoid accountability; in fact, we embrace it. But we also insist on telling you and the public the other things we are doing." Effective accountability systems can include not only annual test scores but also measurements of student engagement, citizenship, and public service. In addition, creativity can and must be assessed if we are to value and promote it. The ideas in this book, including the adult science fair and applying a creativity assessment metarubric, might be a good start.

Forgiveness

The most essential element for a creative environment is the acceptance of error. The Louvre in Paris displays the *Mona Lisa*. Boccaccio's angels adorn the Uffizi. We know the soaring rhetoric of the Declaration of Independence and the Preamble to the Constitution, and we love the *Jupiter* Symphony by the son of that unknown music teacher Leopold Mozart. That being said, da Vinci, Jefferson, Madison, and Mozart all made many mistakes, which, were they displayed as prominently as their successes, would surely tarnish their reputation as great masters.

Policymakers and leaders dedicated to establishing and nurturing a creative environment not only must accept mistakes but also value them. Errors are the pathway to creative success. When interviewing prospective superintendents, school boards should not merely ask, "What are your weaknesses?" and then settle for the contrived responses of "I work too hard" and "I care too much." Board members, as well as the Senate education committee grilling a prospective U.S. Secretary of Education, should demand more. They might ask, "What are your real whoppers? The predictions that were unfounded and the decisions that were dead wrong?" Policymakers who seek perfection during the interviews of senior leaders and settle for nothing less during annual reviews will never learn the art of forgiveness. Any annual review that concludes with "I met all of my goals" is not a reflection of success but of gamesmanship. Keeping creativity alive requires courageous classroom teachers, daring students, bold administrators, and disciplined yet forgiving policymakers.

My paternal grandfather, Sherman Vester Reeves, received his teaching license in 1906 from the board of education of Carroll County, Arkansas. I have never seen a picture of him smiling. It is possible that this is because, at the dawn of a new era, he sat through one too many lectures about the marvelous promises of 20th century skills. May 21st century teachers feel less taciturn and more joyous in their honorable and wonderful profession, embracing and promoting creativity in *all* of their students.

References and Resources

Ainsworth, L. (1998). *Student-generated rubrics: An assessment model to help all students succeed*. Upper Saddle River, NJ: Seymour.

Arum, R., & Roksa, J. (2010). *Academically adrift: Limited learning on college campuses*. Chicago: University of Chicago Press.

Association of American Educators. (2012, April 3). *Report: Art education programs on the decline*. Accessed at www.aaeteachers.org/index.php/blog/700-report-art-education-programs-on-the-decline on February 5, 2015.

Burkus, D. (2014). *The myths of creativity: The truth about how innovative companies and people generate great ideas*. San Francisco: Jossey-Bass.

Colvin, G. (2008). *Talent is overrated: What* really *separates world-class performers from everybody else*. New York: Penguin.

Csikszentmihalyi, M. (1996). *Creativity: The psychology of discovery and invention*. New York: HarperCollins.

Deutschman, A. (2007). *Change or die: The three keys to change at work and in life*. New York: HarperCollins Business.

DuFour, R., DuFour, R., Eaker, R., & Many, T. (2006). *Learning by doing: A handbook for professional learning communities at work*. Bloomington, IN: Solution Tree Press.

DuFour, R., & Fullan, M. (2014). *Cultures built to last: Systemic PLCs at work*. Bloomington, IN: Solution Tree Press.

Dyson, J. (2000). *Against the odds: An autobiography*. London: Texere.

Elmore, R. (2011). *I used to think . . . and now I think*. Cambridge, MA: Harvard Education Press.

Finkelstein, S. (2009). *Think again: Why good leaders make bad decisions and how to keep it from happening to you.* Boston: Harvard Business School Press.

Finkelstein, S. (2014). *The best and worst CEOs.* Accessed at www .tuck.dartmouth.edu/newsroom/journalists/press-releases/tuck -professor-sydney-finkelstein-announces-best-and-worst-ceos -of-2014 on January 31, 2015.

Frank, A. (1947). *Anne Frank: The diary of a young girl.* New York: Doubleday.

Gardner, H. (1993). *Creating minds: An anatomy of creativity seen through the lives of Freud, Einstein, Picasso, Stravinsky, Eliot, Graham, and Gandhi.* New York: Basic Books.

Gardner, H. (1999). *The disciplined mind: What all students should know and understand.* New York: Simon & Schuster.

Gardner, H. (2009). *Five minds for the future.* Boston: Harvard Business School Press.

Gardner, H. (2011). *Frames of mind: The theory of multiple intelligences.* New York: Basic Books.

Graham, S. (2009–2010, Winter). Want to improve children's writing? Don't neglect their handwriting. *The American Teacher*, 20–26.

Guskey, T. R. (2014). *On your mark: Challenging the conventions of grading and reporting.* Bloomington, IN: Solution Tree Press.

Hammond, H. L., Skidmore, L. E., Wilcox-Herzog, A., & Kaufman, J. C. (2013). Creativity and creativity programs. In J. Hattie & E. M. Anderman (Eds.), *International guide to student achievement* (pp. 292–295). London: Routledge.

Hattie, J. (2012). *Visible learning for teachers.* London: Routledge.

Hattie, J., & Yates, G. C. R. (2014). *Visible learning and the science of how we learn.* London: Routledge.

Hugo, V. (1835, September). Scraps of philosophy and criticism. *The New-England*, 9(9), 204.

Janis, I. (1982). *Groupthink: Psychological studies of policy decisions and fiascoes.* Boston: Engage Learning.

Kanold, T. D. (Ed.). (2012). *Common Core mathematics in a PLC at Work™: Leader's guide.* Bloomington, IN: Solution Tree Press.

Kim, K. H. (2011). The creativity crisis: The decrease in creative thinking scores on the Torrance Tests of Creative Thinking. *Creativity Research Journal, 23*(4), 285–295.

Lafley, A. G., & Martin, R. L. (2013). *Playing to win: How strategy really works.* Boston: Harvard Business Review Press.

Lombardo, B. J., & Roddy, D. J. (2010). *Cultivating organizational creativity in an age of complexity: A companion study to the IBM 2010 Global Chief Human Resource Officer Study.* New York: IBM Institute for Business Value.

Marshall, K. (2013). *Rethinking teacher supervision and evaluation: How to work smart, build collaboration, and close the achievement gap* (2nd ed.). San Francisco: Jossey-Bass.

Marshall, K. (2014). *Teacher evaluation rubrics.* Accessed at www.marshallmemo.com/articles/%20Teacher%20rubrics%20Jan%202014%20corr.pdf on February 5, 2015.

Marzano, R. (2007). *The art and science of teaching: A comprehensive framework for effective instruction.* Alexandria, VA: Association for Supervision and Curriculum Development.

O'Connor, K. (2009). *How to grade for learning* (3rd ed.). Thousand Oaks, CA: Corwin Press.

Osborn, A. F. (1976). *Applied imagination: Principles and procedures of creative problem solving* (3rd rev. ed.). New York: Charles Scribner's Sons.

Pentland, A. (2014). *Social physics: How good ideas spread—The lessons from a new science.* New York: Penguin.

Reeves, D. B. (2006). *The learning leader: How to focus school improvement for better results.* Alexandria, VA: Association for Supervision and Curriculum Development.

Reeves, D. B. (2008). *Reframing teacher leadership to improve your school.* Alexandria, VA: Association for Supervision and Curriculum Development.

Reeves, D. B. (2011). *Elements of grading: A guide to effective practice.* Bloomington, IN: Solution Tree Press.

Reznikoff, M., Domino, G., Bridges, C., & Honeyman, M. (1973, December). Creative abilities in identical and fraternal twins. *Behavior Genetics, 3*(4), 365–377.

Robinson, K. (2014). *Finding your element: How to discover your talents and passions and transform your life.* New York: Penguin.

Rogers, K., & Simms, J. A. (2014). *Teaching argumentation.* Bloomington, IN: Marzano Research.

Runco, M. A. (2014). *Creativity: Theories and themes—Research, development, and practice* (2nd ed.). Amsterdam: Academic Press.

Runco, M. A., & Albert, R. S. (2010). Creativity research: A historical view. In J. C. Kaufman & R. J. Sternberg (Eds.), *The Cambridge handbook of creativity* (pp. 3–19). Cambridge, England: Cambridge University Press.

Till, A. (Ed.). (1994). *The collected poems of William Wordsworth.* London: Wordsworth.

Twenge, J., & Campbell, K. (2010). *The narcissism epidemic: Living in the age of entitlement.* New York: Atria Books.

Wanjek, C. (2013, September 3). *Left brain vs. right: It's a myth, research finds.* Accessed at www.livescience.com/39373-left-brain -right-brain-myth.html on January 31, 2015.

Wiggins, G. (2012, February 3). *On assessing for creativity: Yes you can, and yes you should.* Accessed at https://grantwiggins.wordpress .com/2012/02/03/on-assessing-for-creativity-yes-you-can-and -yes-you-should on February 5, 2015.

Willingham, D. T. (2010). *Why don't students like school? A cognitive scientist answers questions about how the mind works and what it means for the classroom.* San Francisco: Jossey-Bass.

Wisconsin Department of Justice. (2010). *Open meeting laws compliance.* Accessed at www.doj.state.wi.us/sites/default/files/dls/open-meetings -law-compliance-guide-2010.pdf on January 31, 2015.

Zhao, Y. (2014). *Who's afraid of the big bad dragon? Why China has the best (and worst) education system in the world.* San Francisco: Jossey-Bass.

Solutions for Digital Learner–Centered Classrooms

The *Solutions Series* offers practitioners easy-to-implement recommendations on each book's topic—professional learning communities, digital classrooms, or modern learning. In a short, reader-friendly format, these how-to guides equip K–12 educators with the tools they need to take their school or district to the next level.

Designing Teacher-Student Partnership Classrooms
Meg Ormiston
BKF680

Evaluating and Assessing Tools in the Digital Swamp
Michael Fullan and Katelyn Donnelly
BKF636

From Master Teacher to Master Learner
Will Richardson
BKF679

Creating Purpose-Driven Learning Experiences
William M. Ferriter
BKF691

Using Digital Games as Assessment and Instruction Tools
Ryan L. Schaaf
BKF666

Implementing Project-Based Learning
Suzie Boss
BKF681

Wait! Your professional development journey doesn't have to end with the last pages of this book.

We realize improving student learning doesn't happen overnight. And your school or district shouldn't be left to puzzle out all the details of this process alone.

No matter where you are on the journey, we're committed to helping you get to the next stage.

Take advantage of everything from **custom workshops** to **keynote presentations** and **interactive web and video conferencing**. We can even help you develop an action plan tailored to fit your specific needs.

Let's get the conversation started.

Call 888.763.9045 today.

 solution-tree.com